WELCOME TO THE FARM
Four-Track Tractor

Samantha Bell

Published in the United States of America
by Cherry Lake Publishing
Ann Arbor, Michigan
www.cherrylakepublishing.com

Content Adviser: Gary Powell, Weed Science Research Technician,
Michigan State University
Reading Adviser: Marla Conn MS, Ed., Literacy specialist, Read-Ability, Inc.
Photo Credits: © digitalreflections/Shutterstock, cover, 1, 2, 10; © Curved
Light USA / Alamy Stock Photo, 4; © clynt Garnham Agriculture /
Alamy Stock Photo, 6; © Tamisclao/Shutterstock, 8; © marchello74/
Shutterstock, 12; © David Wright/Flickr, 14; © All Canada Photos / Alamy
Stock Photo, 16; © RomanSlavik.com/Shutterstock, 18; © Rick Dalton - Ag /
Alamy Stock Photo, 20

Library of Congress Cataloging-in-Publication Data
Names: Bell, Samantha, author. | Bell, Samantha. Welcome to the farm.
Title: Four-track tractor / Samantha Bell.
Description: Ann Arbor : Cherry Lake Publishing, [2016] | Series: Welcome to
  the farm | Includes bibliographical references and index.
Identifiers: LCCN 2015047224| ISBN 9781634710336 (hardcover) |
  ISBN 9781634711326 (pdf) | ISBN 9781634712316 (pbk.) |
  ISBN 9781634713306 (ebook)
Subjects: LCSH: Farm tractors—Juvenile literature.
Classification: LCC S711 .B417 2016 | DDC 629.225/2—dc23
LC record available at http://lccn.loc.gov/2015047224

Cherry Lake Publishing would like to acknowledge the work of the Partnership
for 21st Century Skills. Please visit www.p21.org for more information.

Printed in the United States of America
Corporate Graphics

Table of Contents

No Wheels

Some tractors do not have wheels. They have four **tracks**.

Tracks give the tractor more power. They help the tractor move over soft ground.

Rolling Everywhere

The tractor goes up hills. The tracks keep it balanced. They can grip the ground.

Where does the driver sit?

The tracks move on soft soil.
They go over rough ground.

Working in the Field

A tractor works in a field. It **tills** the ground in straight rows.

The tracks keep the ground even. The ground will not get **ruts**.

Planting Seeds

The tractor pulls a tiller. The soil is now ready for planting.

What things do crops need to grow?

The farmer plants the seeds. Soon they will grow into **crops**.

The tractor will pull a grain cart to take the crops to the truck. The tracks on the tractor keep the soil smooth.

Find Out More

Dorling Kindersley. *Total Tractor!* New York: DK Publishing, 2015.

John Deere Kids
https://www.deere.com/en_US/corporate/our_company/fans_visitors/kids/kids.page
Find links to videos, games, stories, coloring pages, and more.

Glossary

crops (KRAHPS) plants that are grown as food

ruts (RUHTS) places in the ground worn down by wheels

tills (TILLZ) breaks up soil using a piece of equipment pulled by a tractor

tracks (TRAKS) the metal or rubber belts a vehicle uses to move

Home and School Connection

Use this list of words from the book to help your child become a better reader. Word games and writing activities can help beginning readers reinforce literacy skills.

a	grip	plants	they
balanced	ground	power	things
can	grow	pull	tiller
cart	have	pulls	tills
crops	help	ready	to
do	hills	rolling	tracks
does	in	rough	tractor
driver	into	rows	tractors
even	it	ruts	truck
everywhere	keep	seeds	up
farmer	more	sit	what
field	move	smooth	wheels
for	need	soft	where
four	no	soil	will
get	not	some	working
give	now	soon	works
go	on	straight	
goes	over	take	
grain	planting	the	

Index

About the Author

Samantha Bell is a children's book writer, illustrator, teacher, and mom of four busy kids. Her articles, short stories, and poems have been published online and in print.